The Puzzle Master and Other Poems

Also by F. D. Reeve

Poetry

The Blue Cat Walks the Earth
The Toy Soldier
The Return of the Blue Cat
The Urban Stampede and Other Poems
Alcyone and Other Poems
Concrete Music
The Blue Cat
In the Silent Stones

Fiction

North River (stories)
My Sister Life
A Few Rounds of Old Maid (stories)
White Colors
The Brother
Just Over the Border
The Red Machines

Essays

The White Monk: an Essay on Dostoevsky and Melville
The Russian Novel
Robert Frost in Russia
Aleksandr Blok: Between Image and Idea

The Puzzle Master and Other Poems

F. D. Reeve

NQ Books™

The New York Quarterly Foundation, Inc.
New York, New York

NYQ Books™ is an imprint of The New York Quarterly Foundation, Inc.

The New York Quarterly Foundation, Inc.
P. O. Box 2015
Old Chelsea Station
New York, NY 10113

www.nyqbooks.org

First Edition

Set in New Baskerville

Layout and Design by Raymond P. Hammond
Cover Image: ©iStockphoto.com/solarseven

Library of Congress Control Number: 2010907949

ISBN: 978-1-935520-20-7

The Puzzle Master and Other Poems

Acknowledgments

Thanks to the editors of the following periodicals in which these poems first appeared:

The American Poetry Review, The American Arts Quarterly, the Antioch Review, the Seneca Review, and *the Sewanee Review.*

Iain MacLellan, Director of the Alva deMars Megan Chapel Art Center at Saint Anselm College, commissioned "A Girl and Two Doves" in coordination with the exhibit "A Figural Presence," a study of the human body in contemporary art; the poem first appeared in the show's accompanying folio.

for Ralph & Emily

Contents

The Puzzle Master and Other Poems

A Girl and Two Doves

In her soft hands she holds

          two loves of her own,

holds their plump breasts as some day

          hers would be held

now pressed by the birds'

          small, intemperate hearts

hidden in three thousand

          years of stone.

The compassionate birds

          tuck themselves into death,

then withdraw,

          like dockside friends waving farewell.

How lightly her right arm draws

          her favorite closer,

but the kiss of love is no less

          a kiss good-by.

She walks barefoot on her journey

                like the great runner

who, when her parents were her age,

                carried news

of the victory at Marathon

                home to his people,

unaware she would come

                and in her own way die.

What was the cause

                that cast her as stone

so slim she stands

                at half her promised size,

half-faced her form,

                half-blind her marble eyes,

her ravenous heart

                as white and hard as bone?

Pity like moonlight

        drags her famished shadow

across the white rocks

        of the Parian hills.

In the great darkness

        of an asphodel field,

her lost life laced

        in a counter-turned body

beneath a blank sky,

        she dances round and around,

dreaming a long-time lover,

        like the dove

circling the Ark

        holding high the heart of the earth

and the promise of seeds

        garnered from dying ground.

Once she stood in place,

                    a classic perfection,

the ideal of an age

                    like a cameo pinned to the land,

who endured the burning sand

                    of the middle-east deserts,

bitter winds off the sea,

                    the Olympians' defection,

her native hills plundered,

                    and the constellations deformed

by the fireworks of the sun.

Her soul

a loose-draped mourner

in a marble stele,

she bears life in her breast

with eternally ancient charm,

preserving earth's shell

like the crust of a bread

for us as we come

and our immortal dead.

A Push Cart Prize

Where you going, heavy man,

feet a-flapping, worlds apart?

I'm off today if today I can

make love to my girl with my long-legged heart.

Who you haunting, heavy man,

sliding backwards 'gainst the sun?

Streets fly clockwise off the plan—

ain't no more marathons to run.

Hey, old man, you've got square wheels—

two up front, two behind—

Sure, first's long passed, home's to steal—

my honey's halflife lights my mind.

In the Men's Room at the Café Provence

Behind the glass doors of a reliquary

    stacked like the stars

three Citroëns hang on the wall

    above the toilet bowl:

Grandiose plebeian, a *deux chevaux*

    holds the top shelf

like a wax martyr at Madame Tussaud's,

    wheel covers black, body blood-red—

    mascot of the anarchist dead.

Then a screaming dust-covered car in cobalt,

    a princely slim-fendered *quinze*,

roars down the Champs Elysées: de Gaulle,

    his nose, like a clown's, useless at last,

    waves to the crowd of hesychasts.

A gray DS is parked on the last

    shelf: Are days discrete? Do minutes

    make illusions like the lines

Van Gogh wrapped his cypress in?

    Old World steel once-new designs

    end boxed as toys collecting dust

    like bars of gold and Ophelia's bones.

For the Four Thousand

*"The situation in Iraq, with armed militarized
factions fighting for their own political agendas,
can now be characterized as civil war."*
                                    —*NBC News*

soft weather we had all fall

the rain exceeding itself, then hard

dragging the fox to earth

the snow on Mt. Kenya dying

the sun in its fairy-tale setting

      drowned in a blood-red sea

the crèche is umber; blue

for a sky, a dress, a child's eyes;

      no one includes the smell

of the animals or the air

at Golgotha three days old:

      each death draws closer to Hell

bells in the village church

ring the angels' caroling

    glass notes falling like men

such sorrow, so little joy

as if the world were real

    from beginning to end

For a New Year

It snowed on Christmas Day as if to hide

our impositions—boot prints in the garden,

junk cars and broken bottles in the woods.

(Year after year the soft earth partly hardens,

partly blows away like desert sand,

diminished by life like a star worn down by stardom.)

Next morning the children fluttered angels in a row,

then rose like a new year from their cold forms,

their eyes bearing the brightness of the snow.

Violets in a Pewter Vase

for Lockie

As if they were a crowd of pilgrims

    singing in the rain,

each drop complected like the globe

    set in a silver frame,

their music rises from an earth

    that will not stay in tune

so brittle are its longitudes

    and so pale its moon.

The Ghiberti Doors

mira arte fabricatum

I

Coming on a door you turn the knob

to let its musty secrets out to air,

but here you stand amazed at a bronze pair

suspended in the Tuscan sunlight. You touch

and talk of them as if old doors were such

unmoving things an architect could declare

they are but fragments of a building where

a wall opens or a corner gathers dust.

Doors' discoveries can be sensational—

perhaps a royal adulteress caught unaware,

a boy's face pressed to her black hair,

watched by a maid who has a master key.

Here the font by holy alchemy

opens into four concentric spheres

while underneath the gilt entablature

art hangs mutely like an occasional

verse inscribed on a small child's silver cup;

Venus floats forgotten on the sacred air,

and the love you dreamed of, like Augustine's pear,

is taken, tasted, and made up.

II

Imagine the gilt pure gold, liars like Jacob

leaning out for air, the obedient hounds

quick for the hunt, no man caring which brother robs

or what the women think who fill the background;

      down front, showing the motion of her mind,

      Eve right-hands God for the body of mankind.

Tote up the civil gains from then to now,

add alphabets and ships, calculate

the shape of space, the distance to the moon,

the circumference of law, the annual rate

      deserts die and land turns into sea;

      bless the remaining days of earth's orange eye.

As a bookkeeper rubs out wrong figures, for the nonce

the scholars of Florence have scoured time's defacement

of saints' miraculous hopes and people's impatience

that like dirt from the hands of history had overladen

  Moses in Egypt, the shimmering kingdom of David,

  Solomon's justice, and cost Samson his head.

These little men and women in shining bronze

carry on their lives as if there were no end,

blind Isaac pretends to see, and God with a beard

stands tall like a working man. His story bends

  around the earth like light around the sun,

  splitting the air and blacking the space it burns.

THE PUZZLE MASTER

THE PUZZLE MASTER

verse text for a jazz opera

dramatis personae

Delling — a world-famous engineer-inventor

Ingram — his twelve-year-old son

Caribes — a mixed chorus containing all other roles including Delling's nephew Thane, Queen Prue, King Milo, their daughter Princess Arabella, her lover Theodore, and the islanders themselves as commentators and comforters

SYNOPSIS

The setting is an imaginary island in the Caribbean where Delling (Daedalus) has ended up after a fantastic career. The Chorus begins by introducing him and his son Ingram (Icarus) and by reenacting the early episode with his nephew Thane for which Delling was accused of jealously pushing the young man off a cliff.

Scene by scene we then get reenactments of the crucial events in Delling's life starting with his fleeing the city with his son by hot-air balloon to King Milo's island. There Queen Prue lustily persuades him to invent a contraption whereby she can have sex with a bull (which she does). Milo compels him to build a maze for keeping the man-eating man-bull she bears. Each month the king's daughter Arabella then guides a victim in until Theodore appears, slays the bull and is guided out by Arabella's thread. Delling is punished by being put into his own maze.

Although he promised to marry Arabella, Theodore sails away without her, and young Ingram takes up her cause. When Delling fits himself and his son with artful wings to fly out of the maze, the boy seeks to prove his manliness to Arabella and his general defiance of restrictions by outflying his father. Alas, he goes too close to the sun, his wings burn, and he plunges into the sea, where beautiful nymphs cradle his body and assuage his soul.

That brings us back to the present and Delling alone with his conscience on the island, his last stop. The Chorus summarizes his life while he ponders the significance of new information technology for future engineering projects and blames himself for the loss of the boy, who, like his father, "insisted on his immortal right to be free."

The Puzzle Master

The poet's world is a puzzle, full of wonder, full of questions.
—Shinkichi Takahashi

A huge TV screen is the back wall of the stage. The words of the text appear page by page legibly but not distractingly (in gray letters, say) and in dramatic scenes are dominated by colored images—some figurative, some abstract—depicting the action being described.

Caribes:

On our island in the Caribbean

time and space are magic,

where the cleverest human being

may rest from life that's tragic.

The carpenter who built the world

confounded plumb and level;

but our great engineer unfurled

a plot that beat that devil.

We wonder how he rectified

the margins, laid new rings;

how did he carve the earth from sky

and hatch all flying things?

Was it wise to tell his boy, "Some day I'll

fasten on your wings?"

Delling:

When I look back, I see the diminished past
rerise in glory, and my long-limbed boy
like an eagle circle the sweet-contented sun.
Present virtues bleach my old desires,
which, like fish, lie dormant in the mud.
It's a dull country that has no invention in it.
Give me my hands again, you self-centered gods,
and I'll build a circuit city around the world.
Pause
I have small complaints: Meals are boring; the floor's cold.
If I had a daughter I'd sleep with her every night.
If this were my kingdom I'd electrify it. No,
with electric wires I'd cut out holes in its covering,
let the next transgenic generation begin.
Pause
Is this my last island? Call it home wherever
it is. I've always lived here. I've seen men
walk on the floor of the sea, rise up with mermaids
in globes of phosphorous, I, the first engineer,
the maze-maker, the emperor of silence.

Caribes:

Among the types that have landed here
he's not the only one
who's dined with kings and always had
a little butter on his bun.

Men change. Time roller-blades along.
No 'garden-fresh' these days,
so in our kitchen there is none;
still, old-timers ask:
"If you don't mind, may I please have
a little butter on my bun?"

Like frogs upon their lily pads
        and hoboes on their bums
and Diogenes before his barrel,
        old Dell adores the sun.
Don't mind his idiosyncrasies
        or the wild-man things he's done;
he's the one who taught us all
        how to make things run.

First Caribe:
Delling invented a thousand useful things
like the pencil sharpener, the ball-and-socket joint,
the extension ladder, and the submersible pump—

Second Caribe:
Not to mention retractable attic stairs,
refractory bricks and the fire extinguisher.

Third Caribe:
Do I confuse him with Edison and Einstein?
Wasn't he the man who invented electricity?

First Caribe:

Never was a problem he couldn't solve,
never a question that he couldn't answer.
A chess grand master before the age of seven,
magician, clown, a civil engineer,
he's been his whole long life The Puzzle Master.

Ingram:

A turbocharger on a lawn mower, Pa?
How will you do that? Besides,
supposing you succeed, what then?
Won't it take off on its own?
Could I fly away with it instead
of having to mow our endless lawn?

Delling:

My head holds memories like the trays
of fittings in a plumber's van;
the linking plans lie loose on the floor.
Thane, your cousin, whom I trained,
watched the women throwing pots:
"What if the clay turned, not the hands?"
"Damned clever, boy. You understand
the trick of invention perfectly:
text and context interchange;
a rug will fade, the pattern stays."

Ingram:

Why is everyone like Thane
against you? Did he get mad because
you said he was a businessman
and not a real inventor? You said
his cups and bowls were flying out
of windows but his head was empty.

Delling:

I look at you and see myself
thirty years ago when I
was curly-headed, pure potential.
Like architectural elevations
designs of new ideas unrolled
in my unpaginated dreams.
I heard smells. I tasted words, touched sounds.
Each day I felt the air change color.
My arms were bigger than the world.
At night I'd lie on a hill, reach up,
and with my fingers feel the stars.

Ingram:

Everybody says you changed
the world. What was Square One
for you has gone; your Ten's our One.
In school we think in new dimensions.
A lawn mower with a turbocharger,

a propeller on my nose—some day
I'll invent a telephone
the size of a lead pencil and a car
for river travel like a canoe.
'Little Man' you sometimes call me,
but I'm big—I'm thinking big like you.

Caribes:
Ing may want a supercharger
and Dell's got god knows what,
but we're still pleased and proud Thane made
       a wheel for throwing pots.

Delling was no CEO,
       cried, "Who's the master here?
Nephew or not, the shop is mine;
       we harbor no profiteers."

Thane was skilled at distribution,
       which market place was which;
but Delling scoffed he'd merely sold
       his soul to the idle rich.

Now men do things in different ways
       to catch the different cancers
left over from the Golden Days
       when Delling had the answers.

The facts were there for all to see: flamboyant, filled with youthful pride, Thane challenged Delling. Hard words, like stones, rolled down the mountain side; then one day they fought, they boxed, they wrestled, Thane slipped—or, some say, his arm behind his back, was thrown—down to his death on the rocks below. Picture them now circling each other as the argument builds and their well-oiled bodies in front of the forge gleam in the sun.

Thane:

You really think you're a genius, Uncle D?

What makes you think you're different? I do the prep

and all the cleaning, and then suggest the things

that people need. Are you still jealous I

invented the most productive tool the world

has ever known? Am *I* not the genius?

The earth revolves on my simple potter's wheel,

and we ride with it, like on a carousel—

I figured how to put it on the Web

as if the screen were spinning in your hands,

so thousands first, then millions learned from me

the skill of throwing perfect pots. You say

'Exquisite pots of absolute zero value,'

'Empty pots of virtual reality,'

but I say those are the people's pots—

Caribes:

It isn't clear what happened next—

      he tripped or slipped or what—

it's absolutely credible
      he stumbled on a rock—
Delling arranged the funeral,
      delivered weeping, golden words,
so none of us had a clue to go by
      from the master eulogy we'd heard.
When asked if the boy didn't haunt his dreams,
      Delling replied, "A man's hands are his life;
      When he dies his soul flies away like a bird."

Delling:

Nothing can be achieved without a system;
nothing, seen without knowing what to look for.
The world's complex, but science simplifies.
Things should be made as simple as possible,
not any simpler. I'll miss Thane in the shop,
but my boy Ingram and I will carry on.

Caribes:

So many people grew suspicious
      that Delling had to flee;
he packed up all his tools and gear
      but didn't sail the sea
because one morning Ingram grinned
      and tugged his father's sleeve:

Ingram:

Remember, Pa, how you promised us

a trip in a basket around the world?
You said if we had a hot-air bag
as big as a tent the mountain winds
          would blow us far away.
Before he fell, Thane wanted to go,
          and I've been counting on it,
because doing things with you is fun,
like when you fooled the monte man,
          picked up his die and palmed it.

Delling:
I swear on this red heart by my black soul
I never pushed him. In fact, when he started to go,
I tried to catch him. Don't you miss him? I do.

Ingram:
Would there be room for three in the balloon?
          How will you heat the air?
Won't the fire burn the silk
          or maybe some of our hair?

Delling:
Black is invisible:
trees in shadow,
prodigies on the walls,
the cruel sun burning
black holes in the middle of daylight,

41

black holes of doubt and darkness—
The sun sinks at the end of each day,
like a great fish rises
out of the ocean in the red morning.
"Welcome, Sun!" I shout to the noise
though to me it's no more than a warning
of utter darkness to come.
In physics what can't be seen must exist,
but who has worked out the equations for art?

Caribes:
Delling was a smart man,
Delling was a thief,
Delling cast a bronze
that caught up all belief.

He made a little Thane
with, in his neck, a hole
to free, as Delling said,
the boy's immortal soul.

He sold them by the thousands
to all who came to see
the spot where Thane departed
into eternity.

The irony is simple:
although he falsely bitched,

42

Fate seized him by the collar
and forced him to be rich.

Delling:
I am where I've always been,
And where I've been I'm always there;
I unlock the treasures of earth
and reveal the mysteries of air.
My breath propels the clouds;
my tears are summer evening rain;
my thoughts spin worlds around,
words drying on a window pane.
Pause
Past and future surround me like twin islands;
where will I find a shelter? Like a turtle,
I carry my home on my humped back, measuring
the height of the moon that by synodic months
climbs the sunlight through the sidereal year.
I invented the calendar, marked the path
in the garden, notched the column and the sea wall
so at the freshet when day and night were even,
the equinoctial line went down the middle.
I harnessed sun and moon in hot consensual bliss,
destining them to tear each other apart
until, at the eclipse, they dance like petting doves
before whirling off into the endless dark.
Clocks swell and shrink. Men lose fractal time.

The cold, dry constellations no longer sing
the ancient legends I used to know by heart.

Caribes:

Here's where Delling found a home.
　　　　Now he'll put on his prancing airs.
Remember Coriolanus at Rome?
　　　　Or London dancing at Bartholomew Fair?

A man like him will come and go
　　　　like golden fog to San Luis Obispo,
but facts are facts: everyone knows
　　　　that geniuses work *ego ipse*.

Same with women: some try to reach
　　　　out to a man, some often don't;
like turtles looking for a beach,
　　　　once there, some always will, some won't.

*Delling and Ingram travel by balloon, reach King Milo's island
where Queen Prue seduces Delling and then, thanks to a contraption
Delling invents, the king's sacred bull. All this is represented very
suggestively on the screen in gargantuan style.*

Ingram:

The thing I like about
　　　　balloons
is how they get you to agree:

in you go
    up it goes
    then the wind blows
you far across the sea.

What about that island there?
The beach shines white like alabaster;
    down we set
    out you get
    I'll make a bet
they'll welcome the Puzzle Master.
Pause
This is where I really want to be.
How long are we going to stay?
When after lunch you go back to your shop
to get the next thing out of the way,
can I take the balloon up by myself
for a low-level flight around the bay?

Delling:
You'll be my death, you crazy boy.
A balloon's for men—it's no game toy—
requiring serious navigation.
It took us both to get off station,
remember? If the fire goes out,
there's no point in your trying to shout—
you'll fall out of the air like a rock.

Ingram:

But you've done it. We just did it together.

      Why can't I?

That lady wants you. While you talk to her,

      let me fly.

Caribes:

Because King Milo's like a father, and the queen,

whose name is Prudence but everyone calls 'Prue,'

sets the standards for the all-night raves,

our island is the paradise of love.

There's no one she has wanted she hasn't had.

So when she glimpsed a gorgeous bull and saw

his torso and his whizzer, she near fainted.

But what necessity's the mother of

you know—and who's the father of invention.

Ring. Ring. Delling picks up his phone:

"Dear Puzzle Master, please will you help me out—

I can't stand another unbulled night alone."

Then she started crooning: "Last night I dreamed

my lover walked across the waves to me;

last night I dreamed a golden rain on me;

last night I dreamed he lay all night with me."

Old Delling had no Cyrano for backup,

and didn't trust himself lest words,

unlike mechanical devices, trap him.

Delling:

May I suggest that you and I assay
a river walk this balmy moonless night?
There is a cove where when the water's low
the roses' scent is sweet like new-mown hay.

My rude hands soften when they near your face;
the water-thrush and the nightingale enchant
the dark with their melodies of endless love;
the night world orbits in your long embrace.

Caribes:

No matter what you say, the point is
what you do. That held true
especially for Prue, who loathed
her husband for being slow
and boring. "A woman," she said, "must have
a hundred percent love-satisfaction.
Milo," she said, "is a sun-dried carrot
sticking out of the gut of a mealy parrot.
 You're new to the island, but from what I hear
there's nothing you can't invent, and I need—"
Before she could finish, Dell interrupted:

Delling:

Come down with me to the pond where the watercress
sways like a chorus of girls, and the sun-warmed bank

47

opens its arms. The sovereign nightingale,
sweet harbinger of the light, as we rise will bless
two lovers singing on and on,
a man and woman pledged to co-operate
after they've been fitted together in song.

Caribes:
The gentle queen was all aglow
like the evening sky as the sun sinks low.
"Let me remind you, measure by measure,
how Cleopatra, that Egyptian treasure,
had herself rolled in a rug at leisure
and smuggled to Caesar for her pleasure."
That made no dent in his funny bone,
but he realized you reap what you have sown,
so he inquired of the lady what
she'd prefer: a powder, pill or pot?
"*Hic propter hoc*," she quick replied,
"I'm a golden calf at eventide
that like a hinny awaits the bull—
my heart is empty, my purse is full—
the paradox of love I praise:
my stuff is firm these silky days.
Before you call for your pipe and bowl
won't you help the bull dive in my soul?"
Pause
In Mexico men watch a whore

do the two-backed beast with a long-eared donkey.
That's possible since, years before,
Dell built the machine for hanky-panky.
It so suited Prudence and Mister B
that she claimed it as her property.
Here, let Delling tell his story—
　　　　the first part isn't gory:

On the screen: Delling's words and suggestive images

Delling:
She lay inside very like a cow.
She was herself the hot and musky scent
that drew the ravening male, his small mind bent
on violent fornication. The power thrilled her,
and the frenzied threat of sheer possession drove her
ecstatic, as if she were making love with god.
I attached a head and made the shoulders strong
so he who mounted could have his pleasure as long
as he wanted and she was writhing in delight.
Nervous lovers, they first met at night.
She wore a diaphanous gown whose bodice showed
the shape of her full breasts, then opened and closed
with every step, like a tantalizing door
to a secret passage. Her hand on its shoulder, the bull bore
her impatience kindly. The golden tips of its horns
sparkled like fires in the summer dark.

49

Its tail slapped her back the more excited it grew.

She kissed, she cuddled; around the royal park

she led it for hours to teach it what to do.

When it started to prance as if the ground were too hot,

she guided it to the boudoir I had made,

slid inside as a seal slides into water,

and while with a roar it rose to possess what it feared lost,

readied her legs to embrace what she craved most.

Pause

From that day forth my life was cursed. At first,

my small reward was watching my leather cow

quake like a mountain and bellow like the sea.

Then came the curse—her child—half bull, half man—

not mine—I only built the scaffolding—

whose bringing up she passed along to me.

I made The Maze, the prison to keep him in—

and Milo in his rage at what I'd done

put me and Ingram in The Maze, for which

my boy each day laid the blame on me.

Caribes:

In olden days

   they used to say

      Nature gets her due,

but since dot-coms

   have come and gone,

      who knows if that is true?

We shake and roll
        then lose control,
                get screwed while trying to screw.
Afraid of war,
        bored by peace,
                looking for the next release,
we wonder if after Prue
        Old Dell can reinvent himself as new.
Right now he's busy
        'cause the Queen is dizzy
                with her love's success,
but Milo and his pals are using
        circumstantial evidence for accusing
                Delling of having made the mess.

The Maze. Ingram wanders through it, meets Arabella, who be-
dazzles him.

(By the way
        all titles may
                be considered honorary.
At this date
        on our island state
                all royalty lies in the cemetery.)
Milo feels ashamed, betrayed
        by a queen he's hardly laid
                but ridicule makes him scream louder,
whereas our hero of the hour

                    (his fortunes having slightly soured)

                        has chosen to take a powder.

*While Delling talks to Ingram, conflicting images of love and fear
clash on the screen.*

Ingram:

Why do we keep moving from place to place?

Delling:

We don't. We're still on the island where we landed
with our balloon. Remember how we came down?

Ingram:

We didn't. We got caught in an olive tree—

Delling:

You laughed and teased me, but I had a very red face.

Ingram:

So why are we here behind a hedge as tall
as a house with a thick wood fence on the other side?

Delling:

How do you know there's a fence?

Ingram:

                                    I went exploring.

And I met a really nice girl not much older than me
who said to beware of a terrible beast nearby.
What did you make now, Pa, that dumped us here?
We don't have our balloon, and you don't have a shop,
only the tools we smuggled under our coats.
I didn't trust the way she looked at you.

Delling:
You went exploring—new places and new faces:
then think how I love making new inventions.
What you find outside, I discover in.
So, when a queen demands a new contraption,
or a king requires a labyrinth of hedge
and fencing from which no creature can escape,
I do what I can. Truth is, nothing is quicker
or more fertile than the hungry mind,
though greater than the mind is the whole man.
When I watch the sunlight pass across your face
as you lie napping in the grass, my faith
in the future rides high in my heart like a dolphin at sea,
and I understand that what I do each day
is but a mosaic in a grand design.

Ingram:
Is this the fenced-in hedge you made we're in?
But if you made it, why can't we get out?

Delling:

We can; we will—I've already made a plan—

you'd help a lot by befriending Arabella—

that's the girl you met, a princess through and through—

Ingram:

How do you know? She said she's never met you.

Delling:

She watched me while the maze was being built,

and I watched her, because the king assigned

the guiding of the victims in to her.

Each month a man or maiden perishes;

each month she knows the passage more by heart.

Ingram:

Is that what the beast does, eats them?

Pause

You mean,

you first created some kind of monster bull—

Delling:

Not I. The queen did that. Half man, half bull,

a frightening beast that feeds on human flesh,

for which the king then ordered up the maze—

Ingram:

What did you do that put us in it, too?
Arabella was surprised to find me here.

Caribes:

ding
ding
ding-a-ling
ring
ring
dance and sing
one take
two bring
three's the thing
summer's butter
winter's sting
I Ching
late Ming
zing
zing
ping
Pause
That lets in fresh air.
      Verse needs ventilation
like vegetables and flames;
it rots like soft, sweet pears
      in interior locations

when verbs start naming names.

Pause

Tied to each other like two stones in a net
that pulls a fish trap down, Dell and his boy
avoided each other's eyes—Delling, for guilt
at what he couldn't properly explain,
and the boy, for hating that once again his life
was subject to his father's fate. The girl—
she who kept the zoo—the horn-hoofed boy
and its inventor—like a saint soon came between them.
When one day Ingram found a love-note from
the queen to his father, he feared the bull-boy was
his son—his own, unnatural half-brother.

Ingram:

What music did you play her, Father, or did
you sing to melt her heart with love?

Envy—jealousy—the father/son antagonism explodes.

Delling:

                                            Not I.

I did nothing of the kind.

Ingram:

                              You lie.

The love scene. Arabella is nubile, honest, earnest, quick, only a few years older than Ingram. Their passion is pure and direct; they can't keep their hands off each other. They are sublimely ideal and eagerly sensual, so caught in the moment that they have no notion of time. The scene fades into the Caribes' telling of building the wings to lift them out of the Maze and foretelling Ingram's death.

Caribes:

Befuddled by his father's 'No!'

    but sure there had to be a reason

why they were violently thrown

    into—hedge or no hedge—a virtual prison,

that twelve-year-old with a passionate heart

    looked upon love as second nature,

so he read Arabella's smile

    as the tea leaves of his future.

Ingram:

The sea stretches on without ending,
way off, the waves crest in storm;
my friend, we are on a long journey,
headed far from our native land.

Arabella:

Hey, how do you know that? I love it!

    Here's one to set beside it.

Once in our lifetime, if only once
  happiness comes our way, our way;

that's when love's sacred fire warms us,
   and makes us rejoice in the day.

Ingram:
The world is white with apple blossoms
     which, like falling stars,
     cluster in your hair;
each day the sunrise brings the promise
     of love lighting up the world
     around the most beautiful girl.

Arabella:
If my father were much nicer
     we might have never met;
he'd have kept your father as adviser
     and you wouldn't have been set
inside this stupid, prickly hedge
     where I have to check on *Him*—
some day I swear I'll drive a wedge
     in his heart and cut off his limbs—
but I wouldn't be here, either, I guess,
     so we better say everything's for the best.

Ingram:
Do you know there's a wild brook burbling
     from the sybil's mountain spring
down through the wooded valleys, curving
     to the sea where the white waves ring

the island, and little stilt-legged plovers
        race in and out with the tide?
I remember. We saw it, my father and I
        when we were coming over.

Arabella:

I know the brook, I often hear it
        especially in my sleep,
because I dream that water-nymphs
        sing love songs in the deep.
Some day, I dream, they'll sing to me
        a love song I can keep.

Caribes:

The past is like a cliff
whose shadow as the sun goes down
spreads across the town.

Can no young man accept
his father's history? Must he wish
a bolder, brasher list
of heroic deeds and forebears?
Will princes always kill their king?
Will one lascivious grin
from a handsome stranger
steal a golden-hearted girl?
Such troubles in the world—

one man's great adventure
may be another's painful death—
how little the dead are worth.

Delling:
Boy whom I love like a man, imprisoned
with me, like me, through no fault of your own,
let's make ourselves wings and, phoenix-like from the fire
of hate and jealousy rise to what we desire.
Many streams feed the Nile, whose rise and fall
provided priests the natural wherewithal
to calculate the durance of the seasons
and draw up a list of arithmetical reasons
by which to bring the Sun and Moon in phase
with Earth's rotation; our care in building wings
determines if we'll rise up from The Maze.
How primaries and secondaries fit
to wooden bone, then coverts overlay
determine how our wings endure the weather.
At sea the wind is often treacherous,
and thermals give harsh, unexpected rides.
Forget the force that you call gravitation—
all space is curved no matter how you fly it—
many local reference frames together
comprise the global structure of space-time—
but here we have no rockets and must rely
on self and soul for velocity and height.

Hence, the special airfoil I've designed,
the special motion I've learned we can impart.

Ingram:
Isn't this all right? I'm doing what you do.

Delling:
You might file the nib to give it a tighter fit,
lest it be loosed by vibrations of the vane.

Ingram:
I do: I sharpen them and glue them tight.
You do it, if you don't think I'm doing it right.
What about making wings for Arabella?
The three of us could found a whole new world.

Delling:
I told you the physics of the gulls I studied,
like stubborn quanta, mocked relativity.
For every quark and color I discovered
I'd guess space hides ten million in its power.
If like the lazy vultures that loop the air
above our heads, we can last on little food,
we might travel to the Islands of the Blessed.
Pause
You're right: why not add on axillaries?
Once airborne, we'll snap our feet together

61

and stabilize ourselves with banded feathers.
A woman doesn't have a man's pure strength.

Ingram:

She's so light she'll rise like a nymph from earth
and lift our spirits to the Island of the Sun.
If every second the Sun converts four thousand
tons of mass to light and solar wind,
but only fifty thousand kilos strike
the earth each year, how glorious is the Sun!

Delling:

Nothing is grander or draws us closer out
than the water in the sea which founded life.

*So far, Arabella has avoided the sacrificial men and maidens the
bull-boy devours. A dreamy girl, she has stayed wrapped in her fasci-
nation with Ingram and his wild love of her. Now comes Theodore, a
young man disguised as a sacrifice who promises to slay the bull-boy,
to marry Arabella, and take her to his country where they'll be king
and queen after his father's death. On the screen, images of Arabella
and Theodore talking, entering the Maze, killing the bull-boy, and
making their way out are intercut with images of Delling and Ingram
strapping on their wings and rising into the air. Furious that because
of his father he had to leave Arabella without even saying good-by, In-
gram flies as high and fast as he can, while Delling, who looks back,
sees the dead bull-boy and Arabella and Theodore making love.*

Ingram:

Let's be the founders of a new Sun World!

Caribes:

A plot, like gravy, must be thickened;
a young girl's heart may oft be quickened;
the trouble was the bull-boy's diet:
the sacrificers didn't like it;
to put an end to all the killing
they found a young man who was willing
to walk into The Maze alone
and slay the monster or be slain.
One day the girl who had sung duets
but kept a cool head on her shoulders—

Ingram:

As I walk along this path,
            leading who knows where,
I follow like a bee to honey
            your fragrant light brown hair.

Arabella:

You're as silly as a poet
            claiming what isn't true;
besides, a bee'd get lost in here
            and end up stinging you.

Caribes:

—did a one-eighty on the course
and promised to help a traveling man

get the kingdom out of a jam
by guiding him out after he sneaked in
and slit the monster under the chin
and sailed her away in a beautiful boat
and married her under the stars, close quote—
"As long as you're beside me," sang Theodore,
     "I know my life's ahead;
I promise to sail home with you as wife
     when the bull-boy's lying dead."
Arabella then replied, beyond
her age, quoting we don't know who:
     "Problems come and problems go;
     the heart has its lonely seasons—
     some men perish, some survive—
     no one knows the reasons."
That made Theodore wax romantic: "Love!"
     he falsely cried, "I offer you a life
     at my right hand on royal land
     and a soft bed as my wife."
Unfortunately, the urgency of action
overwhelmed the wisdom of more thought,
and Arabella, anxious to escape
and bedazzled by a gorgeous duke of twenty,
fell hook, line and sinker for the ponsi
of a man who did but half of what he ought.
"Nothing I'd love better than a trip
around the world," she joyfully confessed.

"That's my kind of girl," the young prince said,
and pictured them soon on the grass undressed.
Meanwhile Delling, like a parfit gentil knight,
was getting Squire Ingram suited right:

Delling:
Here, your right arm, son. Let me pull
this wing against your shoulder. Steady. Hold.
The buckles. Now the other. Up. That's it.
The chest connectors. The body straps. The guides.

Ingram:
Where is she?

Delling:
                    Who?

Ingram:
                              She wanted to come watch.
If she watched us take off, she too 'd know how.

Delling:
It's not in the watching, son; it's in the wings.
Depending on how you build the wings you fly—

Ingram:
You wouldn't let me make her a pair. You said
she couldn't because she's a girl.

Delling:

> A charming princess,
athletic, sprightly, full of passion, fire,
and imagination, more like a boy than a girl
because indulged by her adoring father
who sees her—after himself—the reigning queen.
Why would she want to escape where she belongs?
Wait. Don't pull. Wait. Hold this, then push.

Ingram:

Where is she? I want to say good-by. I promised
to see her before I left. I have to remind her
I'll be back.

Delling:

> Some day, you think, we'll come in glory,
more famous than the gods for having flown
around the earth? Celebrities we'll be,
praised for having opened up the air
and lifted men's feet off this rocky ground?
Perhaps. I, rather, think of the task at hand.
When you come back, your friend will be much older.

Ingram:

She already is. She's two years older than me.

Delling:

Two years, boy, is longer than you think.

66

It's time enough for some one even older
to turn her head and make her feel all girl,
so she'll run across the fields like a foal in May.

Ingram:

Is that your plan? Is that what you'll do! You can't!
She'll never change! You and the queen had your thing,
but the rest of us are trustworthy and true.
Look at all the times you flapped your wings and crowed
about being on top of the pile, the world in your palm!
And where did we end up but in the prison
you made yourself! No wonder nobody trusts you.
How do I know if we can really fly?
I don't, but we're getting out of here. Out!
And if I really can, I'll show the world
how high I can fly. I'll show her how. Yes!
You invented wings—you invent everything—
but we're going to fly! We're lighter, younger, stronger,
and we'll fly past the Sun to the brightest stars!

Delling:

Check your chest strap. Make sure it's tight. Good.
And the fastenings round the hips and through the crotch?
Once in the air adjustments may be hard.

Ingram:

Listen to me! You're paying no attention,

67

like you did to Thane until his wheel's success
was more than you could take and you turned on him.
Did you push him? No: you were holding him,
but when he slipped, you let go— When I become
more famous than you, you'll do the same to me.
Arabella teased me: "Never mind the stars,"
she said, "I bet you can't fly to the Sun."
"The Sun comes first," I said; "we're going to
the stars." You can go to another island,
you monster-maker, you cannibal lover whose
conniving and ambition trapped us here.
Father or not, you're wrong. I'll fly *over* the Sun!
You want to see? You want to play a game?
Come on! Follow the leader! I'm going first!

Delling:
Wait. Let me. If at the edge I dip
or trip or drop like a stone, know the air's weak
and, as you can, run faster, farther, reach
for that small green island in the distant sea
and let the wind lift you like your mother's hands
when you were small and alone and starting to cry;
or wait for a stronger wind that'll carry a man
like a bird out of sight to the Gates of the Western Ocean.

Ingram:
Hurry, old bandy-legged man!
Hurry, catch me if you can!

Caribes:

Look! There goes Ingram! He's running!
At the edge! Over! Off! He's in the air!

Delling (recapitulating):

He dived into space as small boys dive
on a hot summer day into a granite quarry
on the mountain side of town. He spread his wings
and rose like a falcon in a graceful curve,
where he caught a thermal and, like the prudent bird,
gyred up and up the vast, uncolored sky.

Caribe Narrator:

We watched his easy spiral start its swing
above the breakers on the stony coast,
the green and troubled island on one side
and the ancient, wine-dark water on the other.
While he then circled in a steady climb,
the first human in the history of the world
to look down not from a mountain top
but from above, seeing all there is to see,
his father launched himself, his long, tapered wings
the lifters of his soul, the levers by which
he raised his spirit from its imprisoned past.

Delling:

Although I started climbing toward my son,

I couldn't resist a turn, a backward glance,
and that's when I saw them lying by the pool—
Arabella and young Theodore from overseas
who killed the bull—saw them washing off the blood,
the pool now red like their two hearts together.
I saw the two of them embrace, strip bare,
impatiently touch each other's hair, then cheeks,
breasts, thighs, then soon roll quickly, wildly
on the sweet green grass, then lie there motionlessly,
in their consummate beauty like the dead,
their story obvious to everyone.
I continued circling with my wings out wide
thinking to keep young Ingram from the view.
'We're wasting time,' I thought. 'We'll lose the light.'
When I looked again to see where Ingram was
I saw my son still rising in his helix,
as far above me now as Mount Denali
towers above the continental plain.
"Catch me if you can"—his taunt re-echoed
through the sky, my boy showing off his wings.

Caribe Narrator:
As an angry sea hurls itself wave after wave
against a stubborn rock, so Delling threw
himself against the heavy air above him,
trying to overtake his runaway son,
fearing in his innocence he'd die.

70

Farther and farther away, Ingram rose
as gracefully as a dancer. When Delling looked down,
he could no longer see the lovers by the pool
or his own shadow on the emerald sea.

Delling:
"Take a lesson from the moon," I cried;
"see how, fishlike, it keeps its shining cool.
The Sun, the gamma rays—the heat will take
the temper from the wings, dissolve the glues,
melt the covering that, like our body's skin,
binds parts to frame and shields them from the weather."
The upper winds carried my words away.

Caribe Narrator:
Still Ingram shrank in the turquoise air,
as blue as glacier water, taking with him
in his proud defiance the young girl's admiration
and the breaking pieces of his father's heart.

Delling:
He never saw that, like a sharp-eyed vulture
circling a small and dying animal,
I waited for the end, cursed to live
each moment of his doom, of which I was
in part the engineer. My great wings
took the stiffening wind head on and coasted

back and forth along its threads. I thought
that when Ingram fell, I'd be there to catch him.

Caribe:

The sunlight dimmed The pearl-gray islands lay
like buttons on the slowly blackening sea.
The interstellar wind blew cold and wild;
black ice weighed down his wings; but still they flew,
young hero with the universal dream
and aged parody of wisdom, whose passionate quest
became immortal.

Without his wings Ingram plummeted seaward, landed on a little
rocky island where nymphs affectionately prepare his body while the
Caribes sing a dirge.

Delling:

           O black heart, heart of blackness,
black night in the chambered nautilus,
vast, empty center of his failure,
turn, spin, plunge, bend, reach out—
my wings couldn't break his fall or fold him in.

Caribe:

He plummeted past his father, the wind whistling
through his charred and broken wings. Delling dived
like a falcon on a sweet-voiced lark; he skimmed
the water carefully not to be dragged in:

where had the boy gone down? The islands were silent
like giant tombstones on the wine-dark sea.

Delling:
The shadowy water loosened Ingram's feathers,
and he floated like a fish to the sand
where its small bones whiten, washed by a winter wave
from the face of the earth into the gods' gray land.
Loud, lashed by light, voices rose from the sea
singing a chanty, pointing, chiding my conscience:
"Where were you who turned your back on your son?"

Caribes:
Take him, sisters, from this rock
        to our island home;
there lay him on a velvet lawn
        and strip him to the bone
that the Sun, the father of us all,
        may warm him through and through,
relight the fire of his soul
        and make his freedom true.

Detach his wings and bind his wounds
        and let him simply be
the handsomest young man we've met
        in all our days at sea.
See his gentle face asleep,

how still his two hands lie,
how peacefully his body rests
        beneath the bright blue sky.

Wash him well, then with your hands
        rededicate his plan,
so when he rises in his dreams
        he'll take a noble stand.

First Caribe:

At rest his shoulders show he's proud;
his hips are slim and muscled—how he runs—
and the thick curve of his calves—see here—
propel his caloused feet. Lay hands—
your hands, soft nymphs—his whole elastic length:
how sweet to feel the body of a man!

Second Caribe:

Come, my lover, let's fly away
where the night is warm and the breeze from the bay
brings the scents of an overworked day
and the nightingale calls in its old-fashioned way
        Come, lover, come.

I'll cradle your head in my loving arms
so you'll never again be hurt or harmed;
sweet boy, don't age or lose your charm,

or leave this bed that keeps you warm:

Come, lover, come.

Third Caribe:

So undefaced by death you seem alive

who gave your life for what your heart believed;

who, as we watch, become miraculous

with magic from an older, higher realm;

who draw us out with ancient songs of love;

we surrender to your parted lips;

we bless your broken body with our own.

So beautiful, so lost, your dream forsworn—

a boy's bent legs, bruised arms—a hero's form—

the grand ideal—the courage of a man—

the too-proud victim of a love forsworn.

Child of your age, celebrity of time,

we lie with you in love and peace forever.

Caribes:

Let him, brothers, ride the foam

to our island home;

let him, sisters, walk in paradise

where land and ocean meet

that he may live as our device

for the superhuman feat

of matching water, earth and air

here, there and everywhere.

Delling:

If I had found you, I'd have kissed your eyes

and combed your hair and laid you to rest

as I used to bless you every night.

From my room the world I look on is

a potter's field, bones anxious for mine.

We draw close, son—closer but apart.

A succession of mathematical, geometric, mechanical, and abstract images swirl across the screen, then yield to Delling as he looks back and to figures that he sees, including not merely Ingram and Arabella but also a projection of Ingram as a young man replacing his father to whom the Caribes ambiguously address their closing quatrain.

Caribes:

The ways of the world are eternally fixed

by nature and habit more than law:

Theodore pulled the old traveler's trick

of leaving his lady love in the raw.

Many a girl believes a man

is true who's handsome, dark and tall,

but forgets that when he changes his mind

she, like Ingram, is going to fall.

   Love as it buds and blossoms

   enchants both Mars and Venus,

   but the end of an affair

   shows lovers at their meanest.

We don't know what's coming, see,

because Delling hasn't invented it.
But he has said that he's contented
to read the math of quantum leaps
and forego the structure of complexity.
Words, too, are full of hidden pressure.
The theory Delling's working on
says information is a measure
of the choice you have when, at your leisure,
you send somebody a message.
There still remains the issue, though,
of quality and quantity,
how randomness and regularity
relate what you think 's going on.
Most complex of his life's work
is the puzzle of complementarity:
the world is one, and we are many,
so the quantum equations say;
but every time two parts interact,
all results come into play.
There may indeed be many worlds;
such as ours is, it's only one
but maybe not the only.

Delling:
When I look at my hands I see my broken life.
This line, see, is cut; and this one forks;
and this one turns between the middle fingers;

and this one, like my boy, is creased and short,
caught in the shade of the over-arching thumb.
Pity a man afraid to cast his life
on a roll of the dice—pure chance—or wide like a net
to catch his enemies in. The irony:
the deep-sea'd earth and all its gardens,
triumphant arches, skyscrapers, gold domes,
alabaster cenotaphs, cathedrals,
tall steel cities that at night turn into tombs—
the world was my workshop, my clock, the pattern and
the piece, my library of information
wired to the galaxies of the farthest stars.
If all acts carry out their perfect logic
zero or *one*, *yes* or *no*, connecting
the up-and-down of everything unseen,
then he, too, followed his magnetic curve,
which neither of us knew. Had he lived,
would he alone have electrified the earth?
Would he have laid down a fiber optic equator?
His soul, I think, is a steel-ribbed meteorite
hurtling wildly through unmeasured space.
Pause
Why didn't I wait and train the Sun to reason?
Why not in four dimensions reform the sky?
I had the information. Even the atoms
consist of information, hard core and curve.
"Information," I told him, "is the cause of every change."
Pause.

Ingram *is heard singing a reprise:*

> The world is white with apple blossoms
>> which, like falling stars,
>> cluster in your hair;
> each day the sunrise brings the promise
>> of true love lighting up the world.

> What about that island there?
> The beach shines white like alabaster;
>> down we set
>> out you get
>> I'll make a bet
> they'll welcome a new Puzzle Master.

Delling *continues over it:*
As I said, the meals are boring, the floors are cold.
Where are the puzzles? Don't tell me I've solved them all.
I harbor my losses—grief falls without foreknowledge.
May the jealous gods learn to suffer, too.
May my grief sink in my imagination,
or may I lose my shadow here on this island
and become as insubstantial as a dream.
If information is the universal
substance; if we're children of the Sun;
if I fly with him wherever he wants,
will he love me? My old wood heart in his hands,
will he insist on his immortal right to be free?

Caribes:

The gods take care of death-in-air;
   men, of death-on-land;
Master, there's sunlight in your hair
   and fire in your hands.

About the Author

Born in Philadelphia but brought up outside New York City, a devoted pupil of the poet-critic R.P. Blackmur, and now himself a poet-critic retired from Wesleyan University and living in Vermont, F. D. (Frank) Reeve has long been regarded—to quote Robert Giroux—as "one of America's most gifted and individual poets." He first visited Russia as an exchange scholar with the Academy of Sciences the year before his famous trip with Robert Frost. Recently, he has made his sassy alter ego, the Blue Cat, an outspoken prowler for justice. Reeve's numerous translations from Russian were honored in 2007 when he was invited to Moscow to give the keynote address at the International Conference of Translators of Russian Literature. His dozen books of poetry, his novels, and his short stories about his work on the New York docks have won him an Award in Literature from the American Academy of Arts and Letters, the Golden Rose of the New England Poetry Club, and a LittD. from New England College.

About NYQ Books™

NYQ Books™ was established in 2009 as an imprint of The New York Quarterly Foundation, Inc. Its mission is to augment the *New York Quarterly* poetry magazine by providing an additional venue for poets already published in the magazine. A lifelong dream of NYQ's founding editor, William Packard, NYQ Books™ has been made possible by both growing foundation support and new technology that was not available during William Packard's lifetime. We are proud to present these books to you and hope that you will continue to support The New York Quarterly Foundation, Inc. and our poets and that you will enjoy these other titles from NYQ Books™:

Joanna Crispi	*Soldier in the Grass*
Ira Joe Fisher	*Songs from an Earlier Century*
Ted Jonathan	*Bones and Jokes*
Fred Yannantuono	*A Boilermaker for the Lady*
Sanford Fraser	*Tourist*
Grace Zabriskie	*Poems*

Please visit our website for these and other titles:

www.nyqbooks.org

www.ingramcontent.com/pod-product-compliance
Lightning Source LLC
LaVergne TN
LVHW011429080426
835512LV00005B/347